# Cooperstown
## *today*

**WILDSIDE PRESS**

## JUDGE WILLIAM COOPER

Founder of Cooperstown, and father of the famous novelist, James Fenimore Cooper. William Cooper, who purchased better than 40,000 acres of land, of which the village of Cooperstown forms a part, was a great colonizer. He laid out the first streets of Coopers-Town in 1787.

**JAMES FENIMORE COOPER**

Son of the founder of the village whose famous Leatherstocking Tales and a score of other books marked him as the first great American novelist.

COOPERSTOWN is one of those rare communities which has adapted the best of the modern, at the same time retaining a traditional charm that never fails to thrill its thousands of annual visitors.

The village, with its heavily tree-lined streets, occupies a site originally laid out by Judge William Cooper in 1787 along the entire south shore of Otsego Lake. Very few of its residences are more than three or four blocks from the lakefront. Beautiful estates, summer homes and camps line the shore. Nature has been lavish with wooded mountains, meadows, streams and lakes, all of which form a landscape seldom excelled.

James Fenimore Cooper, most widely known and read of early American novelists, named the lake "The Glimmerglass" in his Leatherstocking tales. Famous son of a famous father, the writer came to this section as a babe in arms; and in maturity, through his celebrated tales, made the land of Uncas and Deerslayer known throughout the world. In the community, and around the lake, names and designations made by Cooper in his stories persist today—Hutter's Point, Points Florence and Judith, the Sunken Islands, Natty Bumppo's Cave, Mohican Canyon, Leatherstocking Falls, are just a few, which are pointed out to visitors.

Col. George Croghan, one of the great Indian agents, deputy of Sir William Johnson, built a cabin at the foot of Otsego Lake in 1769. He was the first white man to live on the site of the present village. He never developed the settlement. In fact he was forced to mortgage his holdings which were foreclosed and the title to several thousand acres passed to William Cooper of Burlington, New Jersey, after whom the village was named.

Because of its position at the source of the Susquehanna, the waters of the lake and river were used during the Revolution to facilitate the expedition of Clinton and Sullivan against the Indians. In 1779 boats were brought by colonial troops under General Clinton overland from the Mohawk Valley to Otsego Lake. At the foot of the lake the soldiers made a large encampment while they built a dam at the site of Council Rock. After five weeks, while the level of the water was raised, the troops launched batteaus on the freshet caused by opening the dam, and proceeded down the river to join the forces of General Sullivan at Tioga Point a hundred miles south.

Many famous men had ties with Cooperstown. The village was the home of Judge Samuel A. Nelson, important jurist in New York State and United States courts for fifty years, ending his career as a member of the Supreme Court of the United States. He died in 1873.

3

There was also Thurlow Weed, one of the most astute New York State politicians of the 19th century, who was a printer's "devil" in the shop of The Freeman's Journal, well-known newspaper founded in 1808, and still published.

John A. Dix was a resident of Cooperstown for a period of five years, from 1828 to 1833 where he practiced law. In 1833 he became Secretary of State of New York and afterwards a United States Senator. At the outbreak of the Civil War, he was Secretary of the Treasury under President Buchanan and is credited with the famous order: "If anyone attempts to pull down the American Flag, shoot him on the spot." Later he was minister to France and in 1872 was elected Governor of the State of New York.

Important also was Elihu Phinney and the Phinney family, brought here by Judge William Cooper to print Cooperstown's first newspaper. From 1800 to 1849 the Phinneys expanded their printing plant until it was one of the largest outside any city, publishing bibles, large and small, text books, their famous Almanac and engaging in general book selling all over the frontiers of New York State. One of their most interesting enterprises was the establishment of a floating book store and library on the Erie Canal not long after that waterway was opened.

Edward Clark, lawyer of New York City, who, with his partner, Isaac Singer, established the Singer Sewing Machine business, bought the property known as Apple Hill in the eastern sector of the village adjacent to the Susquehanna River in 1850. He established his summer home here and was the progenitor of a large family who in their turn developed several beautiful estates in this vicinity. Cooperstown still is the residence of many of his descendants. The family from the very beginning has been noted for its benefactions which in recent years have included the Otesaga Hotel, Village Library Building, Alfred Corning Clark Gymnasium, The Mary Imogene Bassett Hospital and the physical developments of the Crossroads Village at the Farmers' Museum.

The coming of the New York State Historical Association to Cooperstown in 1939, and the establishment of its two museums, Fenimore House and The Farmers' Museum, has focused additional attention on the community as have also the annual summer seminars attended two weeks by two to three hundred people from all parts of the country. Authors, historians and the general public are finding visits to the Leatherstocking Country more rewarding as each year passes because of the Association's activities. A new dimension was recently added to these activities with the establishment of a program of graduate studies. This program, which attracts some thirty young college graduates each year, offers courses leading to the Master of Arts degree in American folk culture and in history museum training.

In recent years Cooperstown has become world-famous as the "Home of Baseball." It was in a cow pasture within the village limits that Abner Doubleday is said to have suggested the first fundamental rules of the present sport. Converting the game of "One-old-cat" (one man against the field) into a contest between teams of equal number was the foundation of baseball as it has been played for more than a hundred years.

At the Baseball Centennial celebration of Doubleday's experiment in 1939 the National Baseball Hall of Hall and Museum which had been built the previous year was dedicated. The original pasture purchased by the village in 1923, was named Doubleday Field. The museum is filled with priceless relics of a century of the great game, and houses the famous Hall of Fame Plaques of great players. It is visited each year by over 125,000 fans. Doubleday Field is the site, annually, of the Hall of Fame game between teams representing the American and National leagues, and is the mecca of thousands interested to see their favorite players.

Persons interested in Indian lore will wish to visit the recently established "Cooperstown Indian Museum" set up here by Clyde Olson. Artifacts of local culture dominate his growing collection very excellently displayed. Mr. Olson has spent many years in the study and excavation of Indian sites, and many of the objects shown were of his own discovery.

Woodland Museum is located three miles from Cooperstown on the western shores of Otsego Lake. It is deservedly popular with its attractions for both young and old. One whole building is devoted to James Fenimore Cooper's novel the Deerslayer. It houses nine near life-sized dioramas depicting the important events of this great novel surrounding a 40 foot replica of Otsego Lake—"The Glimmerglass" of the novel, site of this and other Leatherstocking tales. Winding forest trails, a Bird and Game building with groups of wild life specimens native to this area, a real horse car and car barn, a Victorian Railroad station, a real passenger train hauled by a woodburning locomotive on which passengers ride. All sorts of relics of by-gone days make a visit here unforgettable.

Nor is Cooperstown notable for its museums alone. The Mary Imogene Bassett Hospital, a group of buildings at the corner of Beaver and River Streets, is nationally known for its practice of group medicine. Affiliated with the College of Physicians and Surgeons of Columbia University in New York, the hospital serves—and serves well—a rural area within a seventy-five miles radius of Cooperstown. The first building was erected during World War I and used as a convalescent hospital for war-time aviators.

The Cooperstown Art Association which holds an Art Exhibit attracting entries and visitors from all parts of the nation; the local Woman's Club both housed in the handsome Library and Municipal building on Main St., and Alfred Corning Clark Gymnasium, diagonally across the street from the Village Building, offer other paths to the fuller life for the community. At the other end of Main Street from the Village Building, the county buildings—Courthouse, Surrogate's and County Clerk's office remind one that Cooperstown is the county seat of Otsego County.

Cooperstown has an excellent volunteer Fire Department of three companies. It uses three pumpers, has first class emergency equipment and all apparatus is motorized.

Clubs and fraternal organizations include Rotary and Lions, Knights of Columbus, Red Men; masonic groups such as Lodge, Chapter and Commandery, and many others. The Mohican Club affords pleasant quarters for a large group of men, both active and retired. There is also a flourishing Veterans Club with their own building jointly maintained by the American Legion and Veterans of Foreign Wars.

For the ladies there is the thriving Woman's Club, nationally affiliated; Daughters of the American Revolution; Criterion Club for professional and business women; auxiliaries of fraternal groups; Eastern Star, Pocahontas, National Council of Catholic Women, all offering pleasant social activities to their members.

Churches maintaining strong congregations are Episcopal, Presbyterian, Baptist, Catholic, Christian Science, Church of Christ, Unitarian and Methodist. The Cooperstown Central School serves part of three townships and has a fine campus and two up-to-date buildings. It is highly rated scholastically and athletically, has a faculty of over fifty teachers with over a thousand pupils. and pupils.

It is the lake, of course, around which life of Cooperstown still centers. Lakefront Park, directly in the village, Three Mile Point, obviously that number of miles from town on the west shore of the lake and Fairy Spring Park, a mile up the east shore, offer ready access to the lake, while at both Three Mile and Fairy Spring there are bath houses and docks. To Three Mile Point the swimming classes from the village's summer playground on Doubleday Field come July and August mornings.

6

A beautifully kept golf course, just sufficiently difficult, stretches its greens from the edge of town to the Cooperstown Country Club, a little below Fenimore House on the lakeshore. Motor launches including the "Paula Lee" patterned after a Mississippi River boat take visitors on lake-long tours through the summer months. Sail boats race from the Country Club docks. A little fleet of privately owned motor boats, varied in style and cost, line the docks at the end of Fair Street. Family camps line the west side of the lake. Institutional camps, Girl Scout; Pathfinder Lodge, Baptist Church supported; privately operated Chenango for boys, Otsego for girls, Hyde Bay for boys, and co-ed Ethical Culture.

In 1961 the American Telephone and Telegraph Company established its Bell System Data Communications Training Program in Cooperstown.

The basic objective of this training program is to provide competent specialists in the data communications field in adequate numbers to design, sell, install and maintain reliable data communications systems for Bell System customers.

Between 1961 and 1965, over 1100 specialists from all parts of the United States and Canada graduated from the basic 12 week course; 649 in Marketing, 411 in Engineering and 138 in Plant.

The training program was expanded in 1964 to include a refresher course designed to acquaint the early marketing graduates with the latest status in the art of data communication.

The Bell System Executive Management Seminar was also introduced at Cooperstown. This program is designed to keep Bell System executives acquainted with the latest innovations in the everchanging data communications field.

Even in the winter time the lake is still the heart of the town. Fishing shanties dot its surface, skiers on the slopes of Mount Otsego look down on its frozen crust. The sun rises rosy over the bowl of lake cupped in its hills, the sold ice booms loudly on an occasional subzero night and Main Street always has its quota of pools as to the exact date and hour the Spring suns and rains will clear Otsego.

Excellent schools, exceptionally fine stores and delightful living conditions make Cooperstown ideal for year round residence.

Attractive hotels, motels, tourist homes, lakeside camps and restaurants cater to a quarter of a million visitors annually, who find Cooperstown an ideal vacation spot where history, tradition and nature combine to interest and to delight.

# Main Street

*Aerial view of business section on Main Street. Modern shops and stores, banks and many fine restaurants in this area cater to a wide trading center as well as hundreds of thousands of visitors annually.*

## Pine Boulevard

*Shaded lawns, wide streets, and beautifully kept homes are characteristic of this truly American community. This view is looking west, from in front of the Otesaga hotel and Otsego Lake. World War II monument in foreground.*

## Nelson Avenue

*Another residential street, leading to the Lake.*

*A municipally owned water system plus excellent public utility services assures Cooperstown home owners many conveniences.*

## Cooperstown High School

This attractive building is a unit of the Cooperstown - Hartwick - Middlefield Central School District and cares for 400-500 pupils in grades 7 through 12.

## Cooperstown Grade School

Situated on a twenty acre campus with plenty of playground area, modern in every respect, this building houses about 600 pupils in the first six grades.

## County Buildings

Cooperstown is the county seat of Otsego
County. Buildings included here are the
court house and county clerk's office. Sheriff's
residence and county jail are at left of the
court house.

## Municipal Center

*This handsome stone building houses the
Village Offices, Public Library, Cooperstown
Art Association, the Woman's Club and provides offices and an auditorium for many community activities. It is also the headquarters
of the Cooperstown Chamber of Commerce.*

# Mary Imogene Bassett Hospital

*Affiliated with Columbia University. A two hundred and fifty bed hospital, with a skilled staff of surgeons and medical specialists. Considered one of the finest hospitals in Central New York.*

# Golf Course

*Looking north across the Cooperstown Golf links which lie along the western foot of Otsego Lake, visible at right of picture. Country Club is behind grove of trees in the center of this picture on the lake shore.*

# Country Club

On the golf links facing eastward across the lake, the country club is the scene of constant activity all season. Daily instruction in tennis, swimming and diving are given. Star boat and Comet races are held each week-end.

# Alfred Corning Clark Gymnasium

*Healthful games and sports for all members of the family are expertly directed here. A beautiful swimming pool, squash courts, six bowling alleys with automatic pin setters, basket ball floor and other departments provide relaxation and training for its more than five hundred members.*

# Otesaga Hotel

*Famous for over half a century. View from its front porches looking north on Otsego Lake said to be one of finest in America. Built in 1909 it has recently been extensively modernized. Open from June 15 to October 1.*

*American Telephone and Telegraph Company Data Program.*

*From September through June the Hotel serves as the headquarters of the Bell System Data Communication Training Program. It provides facilities for laboratories to demonstrate and study the latest electronic devices used in business information systems, including communications oriented medium size computer, as well as classrooms, living quarters for the students and office space for the staff and faculty.*

# Cooper Inn

*Named in honor of William Cooper, founder of Cooperstown, and his son James Fenimore Cooper. The Inn is decorated in authentic early 19th century style which blends gracefully with a touch of modern arrangement. It is situated in the heart of the village just a few minutes walk from The National Baseball Hall of Fame and Museum, Doubleday Field, the Farmers' Museum, Fenimore House, the Indian Museum and the lake front.*

# Tunnicliff Inn

*On Pioneer street, less than two blocks from the lake shore and lake front park. One block from Doubleday Field, the Baseball Hall of Fame and the Indian Museum. This Inn has been catering to the public for well over a hundred years and retains the charm of past hospitality with the added convenience of modern facilities.*

# Statue of James Fenimore Cooper

*This memorial to the famous novelist is on the site of his home, Otsego Hall, which was destroyed by fire in 1853. Probably the first white man's building in Cooperstown was Croghan's hut on these grounds.*

JAMES
FENIMORE
COOPER
1789        1851

# Cooper's Grave

*Mecca of thousands from all over the world, the grave of James Fenimore Cooper, of his wife, and of other members of the family, occupies a quiet spot in the beautiful church yard of Christ Church. There's always a well-worn path around his grave which is only a few yards from the site of Otsega Hall.*

# Doubleday Field

*In the center of the village, with assistance from professional baseball, the citizens of Cooperstown have developed and maintain the original grounds where Abner Doubleday marked out his first diamond. Annually a game called "The Hall of Fame Game" is played here between teams representing the American and National leagues. Such a game was in progress when picture opposite was taken. Park accommodates upwards of 10,000 people.*

# National Baseball Hall of Fame

*More than a hundred thousand fans come annually to admire the mementos of the greatest players of all time. Plaques of all Hall of Famers are here. The museum has four exhibition floors and is open the year around.*

# The Village Green

Typical scene at the Pioneer crossroads village at the Farmers' Museum. Shown on the left are the Pharmacy, Doctor's Office, Printing Office, and Blacksmith Shop. In the deep center is the main building of the Farmers' Museum, and on the right, Bump Tavern. At the opposite end of the village crossroads, not shown in the picture, are the Lippitt farmhouse and the village church.

# Farmers' Museum

*Operated by the New York State Historical Association this building is replete with household and farm implements characteristic of frontier homes prior to 1850. Here trained craftsmen demonstrate daily many of the trades practiced in the pioneer days. More than 100,000 visitors come here each year.*

# Fenimore House

Here are the offices of the New York State Historical Association. The building houses an 40,000 volume historical library, seven folk-art galleries, Hall of Life Masks, James Fenimore Cooper memorial displays and many other historical exhibits. Publication offices for New York History, and The Yorker are here. Also headquarters of the annual summer seminars and graduate program referred to on page 5.

# Woodland Museum

*Winding forest trails with labeled trees and wildflowers will add to a child's understanding of nature. There is an Upland Bird and Game Building with habitat groups of the area's wildlife as well as collections of the winter and summer birds of the State. A horsecar, old fashioned carriages, and antique automobiles plus a ride on a 1924 narrow-gauge steam train with two cars show youngsters early transportation. One building is devoted to Cooper's novel, "The Deerslayer;" the center containing a 40-foot relief map of the land around Otsego Lake, Cooper's "Glimmerglass," and nine dioramas depicting the historic tale adorn the walls.*

# Indian Museum

*Traces the development of the Indians in New York State from 10,000 years ago, through the white man's arrival. Top picture is of the central hall with its displays of Indian artifacts of various cultures. Lower picture, one of the many dioramas showing scenes of Indian life. In this diorama two braves are hollowing out a log canoe on south shore of Otsego Lake, the "Glimmerglass" of Cooper's Leatherstocking Tales.*

# Lake Front Park

*Less than two blocks from Main Street this handsomely landscaped park provides shade and cooling breezes for residents and visitors all through the summer season. In the distance, eight miles from the fore-shore line, is Sleeping Lion Mountain, which forms the north shore of Otsego Lake. James Fenimore Cooper called this lake the "Glimmerglass" in his Leatherstocking Tales. This is one of three lakeshore parks maintained by the village.*

# Source of the Susquehanna

*Top view is of the outlet from Otsego Lake, the source of the Susquehanna river, which winds its way through New York's southern tier, across Pennsylvania and Maryland emptying into Chesapeake Bay. Beneath the pines on the left is the Clinton Dam Marker erected to mark the spot where the river was dammed to facilitate the Clinton-Sullivan Expedition of the Revolutionary War. Under the willows at the right is famous Council Rock meeting place of the Indians. Close-up of Marker and Rock are shown below.*

# Kingfisher Tower

Most photographed feature on Otsego Lake,
this tower, reminiscent of the storied Rhine,
adds greatly to the attractiveness of the eastern
shore. It is located at Point Judith scene of
many incidents in the Leatherstocking Tales.
Sailing is only one of the many water sports
enjoyed on Otsego Lake.

# Three Mile Point

*Owned by village and used as public beach and picnic grounds for over a century. Once property of James Fenimore Cooper and often mentioned in his Leatherstocking Tales. Two large pavilions are located here in addition to bath houses carefully supervised.*

# Fairy Spring Park

*Equipped with tables, cooking arches, pavilion and swimming beach. Property belongs to Village of Cooperstown. Shaded by beautiful pine trees grown to lofty heights during the past century.*

## Cooperstown Marina

*Located at the foot of Fair street, two blocks from Main street and Cooper Park and adjoining the Lake Front Park, near the source of of the Susquehanna river. Scores of privately owned lake craft anchor here each season. Scenic trips on an old time stern-wheeler, "The Paula Lee" and speed boats go out from here several times a day. Boat rentals, aquabikes, an excellent restaurant and a fine motel for complete enjoyment.*

# Isn't He a Beauty?

*Many prize winning fish in a well known state-wide contest have come from Otsego Lake.   Thousands of fish, including Lake Trout, Wall Eyes, Pickerel, Perch, Large and Smallmouth Bass, and the usual pan fish, found in New York State lakes, are taken each year.   Winter fishing is popular, and the surface is dotted with heated shanties as soon as sufficient ice has formed, so that the sport continues almost uninterruptedly throughout the year.*

# Winter Sports

King of them all is skiing and Mount Otsego near Cooperstown provides hundreds of enthusiasts with the best. Ski-tows are operated daily through the season and there is a well organized ski club through which full information may be obtained. Skating and tobogganing and snow shoe hikes are a part of the winter program.

## The Sleeping Lion

*Famous mountain at north end of Otsego Lake as seen from a point on the west shore half way up the lake.  Otsego Lake is nine miles long.*

## Hyde Bay

*Largest indentation in Otsego Lake this beautiful bay is the site of several schools and private camps.  Excellent fishing is found throughout this part of the lake.  Site of State Park.*